THE DECONSTRUCTION OF CHRISTIANITY

STUDY GUIDE

THE DECONSTRUCTION OF CHRISTIANITY

*SIX SESSIONS ON UNDERSTANDING
AND RESPONDING TO THE FAITH
DECONSTRUCTION MOVEMENT*

ALISA CHILDERS
AND TIM BARNETT
WITH NANCY TAYLOR

Visit Tyndale online at tyndale.com.

Tyndale and Tyndale's quill logo are registered trademarks of Tyndale House Ministries. *Tyndale Elevate* and the Tyndale Elevate logo are trademarks of Tyndale House Ministries. Tyndale Elevate is a nonfiction imprint of Tyndale House Publishers, Carol Stream, Illinois.

The Deconstruction of Christianity Study Guide: Six Sessions on Understanding and Responding to the Faith Deconstruction Movement

Published in association with the literary agency of William K. Jensen Literary Agency, 119 Bampton Court, Eugene, OR 97404.

For information about special discounts for bulk purchases, please contact Tyndale House Publishers at csresponse@tyndale.com, or call 1-855-277-9400.

ISBN 978-1-4964-7502-2

Printed in the United States of America

30	29	28	27	26	25	24
7	6	5	4	3	2	1

Contents

A Note from Alisa Childers and Tim Barnett *1*

Introduction *3*

SESSION 1: **What Is Deconstructionism?** *13*
Understanding What It Is and Why It Matters

SESSION 2: **How Did We Get Here?** *33*
From Hashtag to Phenomenon and from Deconstruction to Deconversion

SESSION 3: **Why Deconstruct?** *51*
Pulling Back the Curtain on a Deconstruction

SESSION 4: **How Are They Deconstructing?** *71*
Responding to Claims of "Toxic" Theology

SESSION 5: **What Is Being Deconstructed?** *89*
Separating the Christian Faith from Personal Opinions

SESSION 6: **Where Do We Go from Here?** *107*
Working toward Reformation

Notes *129*

About the Authors *131*

A Note from Alisa Childers and Tim Barnett

Deconstruction is sweeping through an entire culture. To many involved in the deconstruction explosion, it doesn't matter where you land, as long as you leave historic Christianity. Some who leave the faith have been deeply wounded by the church. Others feel repressed and harmed by the moral imperatives found in Scripture. For some, deconstruction leads to a self-styled spirituality. For others, it leads to agnosticism, atheism, the occult, or humanism. Still others retain some elements of the faith but no longer view the Bible as a trustworthy guide for life and spiritual practice. What do all these different destinations have in common? The authority of God and his Word are traded for the authority of the self.

Maybe you have a loved one who is deconstructing their faith, and you are struggling to know how to respond. Maybe you are trying to understand the radical spiritual makeover your friend or family member is going through. Maybe your relationship with them has been strained or even cut off because of your "toxic" Christian beliefs. If so, you are exactly who we hope to help with this study.

This study guide and *The Deconstruction of Christianity DVD Experience* have been created as companions to our book. Adapting material from *The Deconstruction of Christianity*, Nancy Taylor and the team at Tyndale have put together a fabulous resource that will facilitate small group discussions. Over the next six weeks, *The Deconstruction of Christianity Study Guide* will help you grow in your understanding of deconstruction so you are better equipped to respond with truth and compassion to those in your life who are going through it.

Alisa and Tim

Introduction

If it hasn't happened to you yet, soon enough it will. One of your friends, a family member, or someone from your church will declare that they no longer believe key doctrines of the Christian faith. They will leave the church and claim that they feel a new sense of freedom. The ground will shift. You will wonder what's going on—not just with them, but with the whole Christian world you've been part of for years.

Sometimes this shift happens gradually. Maybe your loved one starts voicing some questions here and there and isn't satisfied by the biblical answers they're getting. It's a little tremor in the ground. Then a fault line opens up. The answers they seem to embrace are further and further outside the Christian fold. And eventually they post something with the hashtag #exvangelical. A seismic shift has occurred, and the landscape has changed.

Other times the deconstruction seems to be an abrupt and radical divorce from their faith. You've likely seen one or more high-profile influencers in Christian circles post something that begins with words like "This may come as a shock to you, but it's been a long time coming. I'm leaving the church. It doesn't serve me anymore."

These are the faces of deconstructionism. The stories are varied, but they share common themes, and all too often they share a common ending: deconversion. People are leaving their faith behind.

Or maybe you're the one who has been struggling through questions and doubts, and you can't decide if you're going crazy or if you're finally uncovering the truth. You thought you had your faith figured out, but now you're not so sure. And you don't know what to call the phase of doubt you're in, let alone where it's headed.

LOOKING FOR ANSWERS IN ALL THE RIGHT PLACES

We all know you and I can't save people. Only God can do that. But that doesn't mean we are helpless. There is hope for those who are deconstructing their faith. Our faith is built on a solid foundation. There are good answers to the questions people are wrestling with, and there are winsome ways to communicate them.

This study guide aims to lead you on a journey of understanding. First, we'll seek to understand what deconstruction is. Then we'll look at the reasons people are deconstructing. There is a path they often follow. We'll aim to understand the cultural forces at work behind this epidemic as well as the personal crises that contribute to deconstruction. And finally, we'll look at practical ways we can help those who are deconstructing their faith.

This study is designed to be done in community, alongside

other people who are trying to understand what's behind the deconstruction of Christianity and what we can do about it. When we listen to others, we gain perspective on both the questions and the answers. And we know that we're not alone—other people are there to share our challenges, listen to our grief over loved ones who are struggling, and celebrate when we have a moment of understanding. Together we can map a path forward for our own faith and the advance of the Kingdom of God.

TIPS FOR PARTICIPANTS

One word of advice: As with anything in life, you'll get out of this study what you put into it. If you gather each week, watch the video, and have a discussion, you'll learn a little something. Your time will have been well spent. But you won't have gotten everything out of the experience that you could have. If you prepare ahead of time by reading the assigned chapters in *The Deconstruction of Christianity* and then answer the reflection questions after your meeting, you'll gain far more understanding, insight, and resources for thinking through deconstruction. If this is worth doing, it's worth doing well.

To gain the most from this study, you should set aside two or three hours per week for preparation. You can either answer the reflection questions from the previous session and then read the next session's chapters in one sitting or break it up into two or three blocks of time. The time you put into this study will pay dividends in your own faith journey as well as in your relationships with fellow believers who may ask you questions about faith.

When you meet as a group, come ready to share. Your group will succeed or fail based on how open people are willing to be. Come with your honest questions, come ready to listen with an open mind and heart, and be vulnerable with fellow group members. If you have a question or concern, someone else in the group probably does too. Your gracious responses to one another will create an atmosphere where understanding can grow and flourish.

But don't overshare. Your group needs to be a safe place for everyone, and that means you need to hold confidences. Don't gossip or slander people. It's enough to reveal broad strokes of things you've seen or experienced—people don't need to know all your concerns about your wayward child or the church across town that your brother-in-law's aunt heard something about. And while we're on the topic of oversharing, remember to leave time and space for the introverts in your midst to speak up.

General good group manners also say that you should arrive on time and attend every week that you possibly can. It's a way of respecting others. When one person is late or absent, the whole group misses out.

HOW THIS STUDY WORKS

There are six sessions in this study, corresponding with chapters from *The Deconstruction of Christianity* by Alisa Childers and Tim Barnett, and enhanced by their video teaching. Each session has the following sections:

- A few introductory paragraphs to set the stage for what the session is all about.
- **Leader's Note:** This brief paragraph suggests goals for the discussion time.
- **Read:** These are the chapters from *The Deconstruction of Christianity* that participants should read before the next meeting.
- **Watch:** This section spells out the points you should be listening for in the video teaching session.
- **Discuss:** These questions will aid group discussion. They are designed to go along with the chapters you read, but even participants who haven't read the chapters ahead of time should be able to join a meaningful discussion around them. Each session includes at least one passage from the New Living Translation of the Bible, which we've printed for you right in the book. All you really need to bring each week is this study guide and your copy of *The Deconstruction of Christianity*, but if you want to bring a Bible or read from a different translation, that's fine too.
- Key quotes taken directly from *The Deconstruction of Christianity* are interspersed throughout the text to remind you of what you've read. You may want to read some of them aloud during your small group time to add richness and depth to the discussion.
- **Pray:** Both suggestions for prayer time and a written prayer are offered, so you can use either to close if you wish. Ideally, you'll leave some time to share prayer

requests so group members can be supported in prayer as you journey together through this study.

- **Reflect:** These questions will help you reflect on what you discussed and what it means for you personally. Don't skip over these sections; they will help you process your own faith journey as well as understand the journeys other people might be on.
- **Take Action:** Each week we'll work on one helpful action step you can use as you engage with people who are deconstructing.
- **Prepare:** Think about these questions as you read the assigned chapters for your next session. They will help you know where you're headed and what to look for as you read.

TIPS FOR LEADERS

If you're reading this section, it's likely that you've either signed up to lead a group through *The Deconstruction of Christianity*, or you're thinking about doing so. That's great! Your willingness to serve and lead in this way will help others who are concerned about the deconstruction explosion and will bolster your own faith and your understanding of this cultural phenomenon.

We've done everything we can to make your job as easy as possible. As long as you are willing to spend a few hours reading through the chapters ahead of time, can start the video, and then are able to keep the discussion moving through the questions, you're perfectly qualified to be a leader. Here are a few tips and tricks:

1. **Come prepared.** It probably goes without saying, but you need to set the example by spending the time to read and underline the pertinent chapters of *The Deconstruction of Christianity* so you can lead a meaningful discussion. You should be the most prepared person in the room, able to point to pages in the book that are relevant to what's being discussed and answer a question if the group gets stuck. It would be best if you read the entire book before the first meeting, and then reread the assigned chapters for each week along with the rest of your group. Be sure you also spend some time on the reflection questions after each session. Your preparation time will help enhance the group's study and yield additional insights that everyone can benefit from.

2. **Select key questions before you meet—but remain flexible.** If you're concerned that you won't have time to cover everything, decide ahead of time which questions in the Discuss and Reflect sections you want to be sure to touch on, either because they seem particularly relevant to your group or you think they will spark spirited dialogue. Of course, if members of your group want to discuss a different question or you find the conversation around one question is particularly fruitful, you can change course during the session.

3. **Be honest.** If you're not willing to be vulnerable in answering questions, chances are good that no one else will be either. There is no shame in having

doubts or questions—that's how we mature in our faith.

4. **Admit when you don't have an answer.** Some of these issues are complex, and no one expects you to be a Bible scholar. If you don't know something, maybe someone else in the group will. But it's okay—and a sign of good leadership—to say, "I don't know; let me find out for next week." Or even better, "Let's all see if we can find the answer to that for next week." There are many resources available to help you answer any questions your group may have.

5. **Keep the discussion on track.** There is nothing more frustrating for group members than to have group time wasted running down a rabbit trail. And the topics covered in *The Deconstruction of Christianity* offer a lot of opportunity for tangential discussion. Have some sentences ready for these moments: "That's a great point, and I'd love to keep discussing it, but maybe we can table that until after the meeting so we can get through all these questions."

6. **Don't let one person dominate the discussion.** As we all know, the world is made up of introverts and extroverts, and both types of people have wise words to offer in a discussion. However, extroverts don't always notice when they're talking too much, and introverts sometimes wait for a long silence before they are ready to speak. Make space for all personalities to share, but don't force people to share beyond their comfort level.

7. **Pray.** This is the best thing you can do for your group. Throughout the study the group is encouraged to keep a prayer list of people who are deconstructing their faith. This list, and any other requests shared, should be kept confidential. If everyone in your group is comfortable with it, you can send a weekly email of names and prayer requests to encourage one another to pray regularly. In addition, pray at the end of the meeting, reminding people that ultimately the best place to go with our questions and heartache is to the throne of God.

WHAT IS DECONSTRUCTIONISM?

Understanding What It Is and Why It Matters

If you follow Christian media at all, it's nearly impossible to go on Instagram, Twitter, or your news feed and not see the story of someone who claims the label #exvangelical or says they are deconstructing. There is an explosion of doubt and an implosion of faith, and it's happening among our own. These aren't outsiders looking in, but rather the inner circle of pastors, church leaders, and celebrity Christians. And it hits closer to home as well—these are our children, our friends, our spouses. Everywhere we look, people are questioning the faith we once shared, and they are doing it in angry tones and sarcastic memes.

What can we do?

First, we need to listen and understand. We need to

see where these people are coming from, what they are really saying, and how we got to this point in culture and in Christianity. We need to peel back the layers and get at the core of deconstruction. It's impossible to argue against what we don't first understand. And that's what this study is all about. Together, we'll answer the main questions people have about deconstructionism:

- What does the word *deconstruction* mean?
- Why does it matter to the church?
- How did we get here—what's the history of deconstruction, and why is it suddenly so popular?
- Why do people deconstruct their faith?
- What exactly is being deconstructed?
- Who are the deconstructors?
- Where do we go from here—what comes next?

This isn't an academic exercise, though we hope you will engage your mind with new ideas and come away with greater understanding. This is personal. It's coming to your church, your neighborhood, and your dinner table. It's threatening relationships you hold dear. If you haven't personally been affected by faith deconstruction yet, you will be. So it's important to be prepared for the moment when your child or even your pastor identifies as an #exvangelical.

Maybe this sounds scary, as if a whole new threat to our faith has emerged. But as the Bible reminds us, we should not fear. There is hope. There is objective truth. There are answers. And there are helpful, constructive actions you can take to be a speaker of truth and an agent of change.

Throughout this study we've included an action step in each session that will give you practical tools and helpful advice for engaging with those who are deconstructing. The final session will bring all these ideas together. We will get to some answers.

But first, let's define our terms and make sure we're asking the right questions.

LEADER'S NOTE

Your main goals this week are to get group members comfortable with one another, encourage them to begin telling their stories about how deconstruction has affected them, and quell any fears they may have that having honest doubts means they are deconstructing their faith. Begin by learning each other's names. You might ask participants to answer an icebreaker question or share why they joined this study. This is a very personal topic for many as they watch their children, friends, or spouses abandon their faith. You want to establish rapport so people feel this is a safe place to explore the tenets of Christianity and share their grief over loved ones who might be deconstructing. If it seems helpful, you could also briefly touch on the tips for participants on pages 5–6.

READ

Before your meeting, read the introductory pieces and chapters 1 and 2 ("Explosion" and "Exvangelical") in *The Deconstruction of Christianity*.

WATCH VIDEO SESSION 1

In this video, Alisa and Tim discuss the prevalence of faith deconstruction, what it means, and what it doesn't mean. As you watch the video, jot down a few notes.

- Why shouldn't Christians "baptize" the word *deconstruction*?

- What is a working definition of deconstruction?

- Before you began this study, how would you have defined deconstruction and what has been your experience with it?

DISCUSS

1. What are some things Christian parents often do to try to prevent their kids from leaving the faith? Which of those do you think are helpful? Which might not be as constructive?

2. Do you personally know anyone who calls themselves an exvangelical? Describe what you know about their journey and how it has affected you.

The faith and thought journeys of our believing friends, relatives, and fellow church members affect us. That's true whatever direction they go—whether it's a journey to a deeper relationship with God or away from him into what is commonly called deconstruction. If they move away from God, it can leave us feeling bewildered, full of doubts, hopeless, and grieving. In many cases our relationships with them are strained, and sometimes they are broken beyond repair. We need to have something to bolster our own faith even as we make space for the honest questions and doubts Christians have about their faith. And we need better answers. Most importantly, we need to understand what's really going on and what's at stake.

> The weapons of our warfare are not of the flesh but have divine power to destroy strongholds. We destroy arguments and every lofty opinion raised against the knowledge of God, and take every thought captive to obey Christ.
>
> 2 CORINTHIANS 10:4-5, ESV

The fundamental nature of spiritual warfare is not power encounters; it's truth encounters.[1] *It's a battle of* ideas.

The Deconstruction of Christianity, page 10

3. Based on 2 Corinthians 10:4-5, how would you define spiritual warfare? How does the battle of ideas fit into your understanding of spiritual warfare?

Read Ephesians 6:10-20:

A final word: Be strong in the Lord and in his mighty power. Put on all of God's armor so that you will be able to stand firm against all strategies of the devil. For we are not fighting against flesh-and-blood enemies, but against evil rulers and authorities of the unseen world, against mighty powers in this dark world, and against evil spirits in the heavenly places.

Therefore, put on every piece of God's armor so you will be able to resist the enemy in the time of evil. Then after the battle you will still be standing firm. Stand your ground, putting on the belt of truth and the body armor of God's righteousness. For shoes, put on the peace that comes from the Good News so that you will be fully prepared. In addition to all of these, hold up the shield of faith to stop the fiery arrows of the devil. Put on salvation as your helmet, and take the sword of the Spirit, which is the word of God.

Pray in the Spirit at all times and on every occasion. Stay alert and be persistent in your prayers for all believers everywhere.

And pray for me, too. Ask God to give me the right words so I can boldly explain God's mysterious plan that the Good News is for Jews and Gentiles alike. I am in chains now, still preaching this message as God's ambassador. So pray that I will keep on speaking boldly for him, as I should.

EPHESIANS 6:10-20

4. What does Ephesians 6 add to your understanding of
   spiritual warfare?

5. How can we engage in the battle for truth in the arena
   of ideas, using the armor of God? What weapons
   are particularly necessary when we are dealing with
   deconstruction?

We all have questions. In fact, part of growing in our faith
requires asking questions of God, the Bible, and ourselves. It
can be scary to admit what we don't know, and that is why
some people shy away from it, but throughout Scripture we
see examples of godly men and women asking hard questions. God can handle it. He knows that this is how we grow
in our relationship with him. So where is the line between
healthy curiosity and a quest for truth versus deconstruction
and deconversion? Let's explore that a little bit.

6. What are some questions you have about the Bible or the Christian faith?

7. In the following list, circle the questions or statements you think are a common or healthy part of the faithful Christian experience. Then underline the ones you would say are evidence of someone who is not yet a believer or is in the process of deconstructing their faith.

a. Why is evil allowed to continue in the world?

b. How can a good God allow war?

c. You can't really know what the Bible means. Everyone interprets it in their own way.

d. The Bible is just a human book, and that's why it has so many errors and contradictions.

e. The Bible has some things that seem contradictory, and I don't understand how they fit together.

f. Does God condone genocide?

g. Is God good? Can I trust him?

h. Jesus was just a good teacher, and he didn't rise from the dead.

    i.   Miracles can't happen. When you see those in the Bible, they can either be explained as natural phenomena or are exaggerations.

    j.   Some things in the Bible might not be literally true, but they are still meaningful and real.

8. People in the Bible asked some of the questions listed above, and they were not reprimanded for it. Clearly it's okay to have questions and wrestle through things. What is the difference between asking a difficult question and deconstruction? If you imagine a spectrum between honest doubts and questions versus deconversion, where would you say your questions fall? Draw an X on the line below to mark the spot.

_____

Honest doubt   Deconversion

Asking your hard questions, correcting your false beliefs, and facing your deepest doubts are all a natural part of maturing as a Christian.

The Deconstruction of Christianity, page 12

9. Do you think there is a good kind of deconstruction?
   If so, what does it entail? What would characterize bad
   deconstruction?

Deconstruction, as culture defines it, is at odds with Christianity. It is not about correct theology; it is about rejection of the authority of the Bible. It is not about arriving at objective truth but rather about living your own "truth." And it is not based on any external authority but rather is defined solely by the self.

Deconstruction is not *about getting your theology right. It's* not *about trying to make your views match reality. It's about tearing down doctrines that are morally wrong* to you *to make them match your own internal conscience, moral compass, true authentic self, or whatever else it's being called these days.*

The Deconstruction of Christianity, page 25

   Alisa and Tim came to the conclusion that the word *deconstruction* should not be used to describe a healthy process because (1) culture defines the word as a rejection of Scripture as an objective standard of truth, so using the word another way comes across to the deconstruction community as deceptive; (2) it is cringey, awkward, and confusing when we sacrifice clarity in an attempt to be relevant; and (3) the philosophical baggage of the word *deconstruction* is too great to overcome. For these reasons, we will move forward in this study of deconstruction drawing a firm line between doubt and deconstruction.

If you are asking honest questions in good faith, with the Bible as your standard for truth and with a desire to know God better, you are not deconstructing. You may have doubts; that is normal—even people in the Bible expressed doubt, and they were not criticized for it. You may be trying to separate things you were taught about Christianity that are primarily cultural from what the Bible actually says. That's a good thing. Living out the life of faith with honesty and integrity involves asking some hard questions and growing in our understanding of God and his Word.

What separates a doubter from a deconstructionist is their view of Scripture. Do you believe that God's Word is an authoritative and objective standard of truth? Do you at least seek to discover if the Bible is reliable and authoritative? If so, your questions will help you reconstruct on the bedrock of truth. This study will help you understand your faith better and respond well to the arguments of deconstructionists.

Faith deconstruction is a postmodern process of rethinking your faith without regarding Scripture as a standard.

The Deconstruction of Christianity, page 26

When we use the word deconstructionist, *we are talking specifically about the most influential voices online who are actively attempting to dismantle historic Christianity, discredit the church, and promote an atmosphere of faith deconstruction.*

The Deconstruction of Christianity, page 27

10. Chapter 2 opens with some #exvangelical quotes, including these:

- "A god that requires belief in it in order to avoid eternal punishment while also not providing evidence of its existence is not a loving god." #exvangelical[2]
- "I'm not going to derive my cosmology from four-thousand-year-old legends of a jealous, bloodthirsty demigod." #exvangelical[3]
- "In abusive relationships, one person convinces another person that they are worthless and no one else could ever love them. That's why people stay. This is also how the church operates." #exvangelical[4]

What similar quotes, statements, or sentiments have you encountered? What generalizations and assumptions are people who say these things making about evangelical Christianity? What do you think is the goal of those making these statements?

> *The one thing virtually all deconstruction stories have in common is what they say they are leaving behind.*
>
> *The Deconstruction of Christianity*, page 30

11. What are common beliefs about what *evangelical* means? What do you think it means?

People define *evangelical* in somewhat varied ways, but there are some common themes, and it is these core doctrines that those who are deconstructing reject. Deconstructionist Blake Chastain has written that exvangelicals are leaving behind

- a literal reading of the Bible,
- a belief that women are to be submissive to men,
- a belief in the sanctity of heterosexuality/ heteronormativity and a rejection of homosexuality as sinful,
- the assumption that the American way of life is best, and
- identification and partnership with political and social conservatism.[5]

12. Let's take a closer look at several of the bullet points on page 26.

    a. What does it mean to interpret the Bible literally? What does it not mean?

In the deconstruction movement, rejecting a "literal reading" of the Bible often means rejecting the idea that the text has a literal, objective meaning the Christian needs to discover and accept. Biblical interpretation becomes subjective, or the Bible is rejected altogether.

The Deconstruction of Christianity, page 35

    b. Faithful Christians disagree on the specifics of what the Bible says about women and what that means in the life of a believer. Putting all that aside, what are some things the Bible does *not* say about women that are often held up as a caricature or straw man that many deconstructionists tear down?

c. In simple terms, the Bible teaches that God made two sexes—men and women—in his image, and that the design for marriage is one man and one woman for life. According to the Bible, any sexual activity outside of this is immoral. Very briefly, what does God's design for sex and marriage communicate about our identity and the purpose of sex? How is this opposed to what culture says about our identity and the purpose of sex?

d. God stands above every earthly government. But our faith should not be separate from our political views, just as it should not be separate from any other area of life. Without debating a particular political position (and understanding that thinking Christians can disagree on certain political points), describe how your political views are shaped or influenced by your faith.

For Christians, politics will flow downstream from theology. In other words, how we vote and engage politically will be informed by what we believe about God and what he says in his Word.

The Deconstruction of Christianity, page 39

13. Do you think *evangelical* is a helpful term? In what ways are you uncomfortable with that label?

PRAY

Close your time together with prayer. Invite group members to share briefly about their struggles, particularly as they pertain to deconstruction. You might want to keep a list of family members and friends for whom people are praying as they work to understand the deconstructionist movement. Prayer requests must be kept confidential in the group. End your time with a simple prayer such as the one below:

Dear heavenly Father,

The topics we've discussed are heavy on our hearts. We are so sad to see people moving from honest doubt to faith deconstruction. We pray for your protection over the hearts and minds of those we love. Help them to see truth and to know you intimately. We pray for your wisdom as we continue to learn and think and process the struggles of deconstruction. You are the Light of the World and the source of all truth. Help us to understand and walk in the truth. Amen.

REFLECT

Before the next group meeting, take some time to reflect on what was discussed this week and how to put it into practice.

- What are some questions you have about your faith or about the deconstruction movement that you hope to gain clarity on through this study?

- Review the five ideas on page 26 of this guide that exvangelicals tend to be leaving behind. Which ones are you less familiar with or unsure of your position on? Where could you find more information about what the Bible says on these topics?

- Some deconstructionists say they are looking for revival. What kind of revival are you praying for?

TAKE ACTION

We are not helpless victims of deconstruction. There are helpful, healthy actions we can take to fight this spiritual battle, and each week we will add one action step to our armory. By the end of these six sessions, you will know how you can be a proactive ambassador for truth. Along the way, these action steps will increase your compassion for and understanding of those who are deconstructing their faith. This week the action step is simply to **pray**.

- Add people you know who are deconstructing to your prayer list and pray for them daily. Ask that God would open their eyes to truth. Ask for wisdom in your interactions with them. Ask for God to increase your love for them and help you express love to them in healthy ways.
- Pray that your own understanding of faith deconstruction would grow through this study. Pray that God would reveal the truth to you.
- Pray in faith. Use passages such as Ephesians 1:16-20 or Jude 1:20-25 to inform your prayers.

- Pray for your church and the universal church to stand strong against the false doctrines and faithlessness of deconstruction. Ask God how he might be calling you to engage with these issues more publicly.

PREPARE

Session 2 covers chapters 3 and 4 ("Rerun" and "Fallout") in *The Deconstruction of Christianity*. Read those chapters in preparation for your next meeting. As you read, think about these questions:

- What aspects of deconstruction have we seen before in philosophical or theological ideologies?

- How has faith deconstruction affected you and your faith journey? What makes this personal for you?

HOW DID WE GET HERE?

*From Hashtag to Phenomenon
and from Deconstruction to Deconversion*

It seems as if every day another big-name Christian has deconstructed their faith. How did it become so prevalent, when twenty years ago it was very rare for a prominent Christian to lose their faith? Is this a passing fad we just need to wait out, a contagion that will burn itself out, or a key battle against the forces of darkness that we must fight and win?

The truth is, none of this is original. The words may be new, the terms *deconstruction* and *exvangelical* may sound fresh, but the ideas behind them date back to Satan's temptation in the Garden of Eden. Satan is recycling the same old lines and the same old lies. He's using worn-out tactics because they still work. Our struggles and doubts may feel very personal, but they are part of the human experiences of doubt and suffering that are as old as time.

Satan whispers today, just as he whispered to Eve, *Did*

*God really say that? That isn't what he meant. Look how appeal-
ing these other philosophies are—they don't ask you to sacrifice
anything or obey anyone but yourself.* He tempts us to deconstruct what God says to the point where we believe so many
lies about him that we reject him. All too often people eat
the fruit and suffer the consequences.

The more we can understand the mind of God and separate it from the lies of Satan as he speaks through culture
and false ideologies, the more we will be able to stand for
truth and walk in faith. In this endeavor, we have guidance.
God's Word lights our way, and the Holy Spirit leads us into
truth. If we listen to the voice of our Good Shepherd, we
hear the truth that will clear away the confusion and chaos
of deconstruction.

LEADER'S NOTE

Your main goals this week are to continue to (1) create a
healthy place for people to explore challenging topics and
possibly disagree and (2) help participants understand the
false teaching and cultural influences behind deconstruction
so they can begin to see how individuals move from grappling with ideas to deconverting. You'll want to create an
atmosphere of openness and a tone of hope as you discuss
what is often a heartbreaking topic.

READ

Before your meeting, read chapters 3 and 4 ("Rerun" and
"Fallout") in *The Deconstruction of Christianity.*

WATCH VIDEO SESSION 2

In this video, Alisa and Tim discuss the origins of deconstruction—how we got here—as well as the more personal side of how deconstruction affects us. As you watch the video, jot down a few notes.

- What is the common story or process of deconstruction?

- What are the two sides to deconstruction that require different responses?

- How have you seen the process of deconstruction work out among your friends or family?

DISCUSS

1. We talked last session about the difference between doubt and deconstruction and encouraged each other to ask good questions as we engage with truth. What questions have been on your mind this week as you've considered your own faith journey, interacted with others, or thought about what you're learning in this study?

Read Genesis 3:1-7. We want to identify in the passage the progression from *deconstructed idea* to *disobedient deed*.

> The serpent was the shrewdest of all the wild animals the LORD God had made. One day he asked the woman, "Did God really say you must not eat the fruit from any of the trees in the garden?"
>
> "Of course we may eat fruit from the trees in the garden," the woman replied. "It's only the fruit from the tree in the middle of the garden that we are not allowed to eat. God said, 'You must not eat it or even touch it; if you do, you will die.'"
>
> "You won't die!" the serpent replied to the

woman. "God knows that your eyes will be opened as soon as you eat it, and you will be like God, knowing both good and evil."

The woman was convinced. She saw that the tree was beautiful and its fruit looked delicious, and she wanted the wisdom it would give her. So she took some of the fruit and ate it. Then she gave some to her husband, who was with her, and he ate it, too. At that moment their eyes were opened, and they suddenly felt shame at their nakedness. So they sewed fig leaves together to cover themselves.

GENESIS 3:1-7

2. What was Satan really doing in his first question— what is the implication behind the question he asks?

Not all questions are honest *questions. When it comes to faith, some questions seek answers, and some questions seek exits. There are questions that seek after truth, but other questions seek to avoid truth.*

The Deconstruction of Christianity, page 44

3. What are some examples of questions that seem to seek exits rather than answers? What are some characteristics of these kinds of dishonest questions that can help us recognize them?

4. What was Satan trying to do by telling Eve that she wouldn't die if she ate the forbidden fruit and that "God knows that your eyes will be opened . . . and you will be like God"? What are some examples of this tactic in culture today?

5. What truths about God's character does Satan deconstruct in his interaction with Eve? What does this say about how people are tempted to move from doubt to deconstruction? How have you seen this play out in real life?

Satan isn't the only one who can affect your view of God—your life experiences shape it as well. This can be either positive or negative, depending on how closely the influences align with biblical truth. For example, your understanding of God as your Father is influenced by your own experience of earthly fathers. Likewise, your assumptions about worship may be shaped by your church's customs. And like it or not, the messages in culture and media also play a role in your view of faith, the character of God, and what it means to be a Christian.

We are all prone to imagine a god that is more like our culture (or ourselves) than who God truly is. If we're not careful, this can distort our view of him.

The Deconstruction of Christianity, page 49

6. How has culture shaped your view of God and the Christian faith? Is this all negative, or are there some positives to the way culture interacts with your view of God?

7. How can Christians engage with people of other religions without being overly influenced by their worldviews? How have you personally engaged with someone of a different faith background?

Christians are influenced by culture, but we are also able to influence culture. It's a two-way street. The key is to be intentional about developing a biblical worldview and then have a plan for how to communicate it by our actions and our words.

The only way to guard against false ideas about God is to fill our minds with true ideas about him. But thinking rightly about God doesn't come naturally.

The Deconstruction of Christianity, page 53

There is an incontrovertible and direct link between knowing God and loving him. We simply can't love him if we don't know him. And if we truly know him, we will love him. Knowing God requires intentionality and effort. Fortunately, he makes it easier for us—he is a God who reveals himself through word and deed on every page of the Bible. He doesn't just tell us that he is love; he shows us what that means.

8. What habits or practices are you engaging in to help you fill your mind with true ideas about God? What habits or practices would you like to start developing?

9. What are some things you understand about love from knowing God that you would not know any other way? Or to put it another way, what is it about God's love that is different from the world's version of love?

According to the Word of God, it's not loving to affirm or celebrate something that is sinful, harmful, or untrue. This is the opposite of our culture's definition of love, which is more along the lines of accepting, affirming, and celebrating whatever someone deems as "their truth."

The Deconstruction of Christianity, page 50

10. How can Christians proactively help to shape culture's definition of love? How can you do this in your family? Among your friends? In your workplace? Online?

11. How might shaping the culture in your spheres of influence help safeguard others against faith deconstruction?

12. Think back to the story of the golden calf in Exodus 32 (or look it up and reread it). What parallels do you see between the golden calf and modern-day faith deconstruction? What does this story teach us about the true nature and cause of deconstruction and what to do about it?

Let's recap. Satan's temptation of Eve in the Garden was the first deconstruction, and the same scenario continues to play out today in a familiar pattern when Christians

- follow cultural norms and allow them to influence their beliefs,
- lose knowledge of (and love for) God,
- prioritize personal preferences over objective truth, and
- are more in love with the world than with God.

This can feel like a very private journey, but it isn't. Deconstruction affects not only the person who is going on the journey away from faith—it impacts everyone who cares about them as well. We are the body of Christ, and when one part is cut off, it hurts!

When deconstruction leads to a rejection of faith, that can feel like a death both to the one deconstructing and to their loved ones. Like physical death, deconstruction can leave loved ones shocked, confused, and grieving.

The Deconstruction of Christianity, page 66

It can be heartbreaking to watch someone we love or trust go through faith deconstruction. It feels like a death or divorce, and in many ways the grief is similar. Know that you are not alone in your sorrow. Jesus walks beside you and brings comfort.

13. How has someone else's deconstruction affected you? What does it feel like to watch a person deconstruct their faith?

14. Engaging with the deconstruction of others involves having tears in our eyes and a sword in our hand—it is both a burial and a battle.

    a. How can we navigate the two approaches, especially when this is a deeply personal issue?

    b. How does each approach affect what we say when engaging with someone in deconstruction?

c. How do we know which type of reaction (grief versus active opposition) is called for in a particular scenario or interaction?

15. Read 2 Timothy 3:1-7, which begins below. How does knowing that Scripture predicted a time when people would turn from God help you deal with it better?

You should know this, Timothy, that in the last days there will be very difficult times. For people will love only themselves and their money. They will be boastful and proud, scoffing at God, disobedient to their parents, and ungrateful. They will consider nothing sacred. They will be unloving and unforgiving; they will slander others and have no self-control. They will be cruel and hate what is good. They will betray their friends, be reckless, be puffed up with pride, and love pleasure rather than God. They will act religious, but they will reject the power that could make them godly. Stay away from people like that!

They are the kind who work their way into people's homes and win the confidence of vulnerable women who are burdened with the guilt of sin and controlled by various desires. (Such women are forever following new teachings, but they are never able to understand the truth.)

2 TIMOTHY 3:1-7

We are not attempting to destroy people. Rather, as 2 Corinthians 10:4-5 says, we want to destroy the ideas that would seek to enslave people to false understandings of God—to help them, instead, to "continue in the things [they] have learned and become convinced of," the things taught by inspired Scripture (2 Timothy 3:14-17, NASB).

PRAY

Close your time together with prayer. Invite group members to share briefly about their struggles and sorrows, particularly as they pertain to deconstruction. As a group, lift up those family members and friends whom people are praying for and walking alongside as they try to understand the deconstructionist movement. (Prayer requests shared must be kept confidential in the group.) End your time with a simple prayer such as the that follows:

Dear heavenly Father,

You know how difficult it can be to battle against the lies of Satan and engage with the culture we live in. We are sometimes tempted to believe things that are not true and to doubt your goodness. Help us to know you and love you so that we can walk in truth. Help us to engage with our disbelieving friends and neighbors, to show them your love, and to speak truth in the face of lies. Help us to be loving and kind in the way we interact with others. Comfort our broken hearts as we watch people we love struggle, and give us the gift of discernment. Amen.

REFLECT

Before the next group meeting, take some time to reflect on what was discussed this week and how to put it into practice.

- Where do your beliefs look more like the world than God's Word? Think particularly about
  - » how you define love,
  - » how you determine right and wrong, and
  - » how you define God's blessing.

- Though they once ministered together, there was a big difference between the trajectory of Demas, who left the faith because he was "in love with this present world" (2 Timothy 4:10, ESV) and the apostle Paul, who "fought the good fight . . . finished the race . . . [and] kept the faith" (2 Timothy 4:7-8, ESV). Which one more accurately describes where you are headed if you continue on the path you are currently on? Meditate on Matthew 16:24 (below) as you ponder your answer.

Jesus said to his disciples, "If any of you wants to be my follower, you must give up your own way, take up your cross, and follow me."

MATTHEW 16:24

TAKE ACTION

Keep praying for those you know who are deconstructing, and add the second action step: **Stay calm.** It can be scary to hear the lies people are believing and to see the p that culture is heading toward. But the best way to counter all of that is to stay calm and engage with it. This week, have a conversation with someone who identifies as a deconstructor or exvangelical. Don't attack them with truth. In fact, in the beginning, it is best if you don't say much at all—simply ask questions and listen with a compassionate heart. There will come a time to speak truth, but first you have to attempt to create a safe relationship where the other person feels free to share. See if you can begin to figure out the answers to these questions:

- What does this person mean when they talk about questioning or deconstructing their faith? Is your friend or loved one open about their deconstruction, or is it something you are detecting through their comments, attitude, social media posts, and/or body language?

- What experiences put them on this path?

- Are there places where their thought process is flawed or illogical?

PREPARE

Session 3 covers chapters 5 and 6 ("Crisis" and "Upper Story") in *The Deconstruction of Christianity*. Read those chapters in preparation for your next meeting. As you read, think about these questions:

- What factors might lead one person to deconstruct and another to reconstruct their faith despite coming from the same family, church, or faith background?

- What are the practical implications of confining religion and morality to the category of "upper-story" truth?

WHY DECONSTRUCT?

Pulling Back the Curtain on a Deconstruction

People don't deconstruct in a vacuum. They are influenced by the things they read, the voices they listen to, and the experiences they have. So if we want to help point people to truth, we need to understand how they got to where they are. And that begins with having compassion for their stories. It's not enough to understand that these struggles and temptations are as old as time. We also must understand the specific triggers and cultural moments that characterize today's deconstruction movement and how they have impacted the hearts and minds of the specific people we are interacting with.

Of course, the triggers aren't the full story. We all face challenges to our faith, and some of us emerge with our faith intact while others do not. What makes the difference? There are two key factors at work: what kind of faith foundation the person is building on and how they define truth.

If an individual's roots grow deep into God's Word, they will understand the truth claims Jesus is making and believe them. There is only one way to be made right with God, and that is through faith in his Son, Jesus Christ. Anyone who believes in Jesus is forgiven and saved. But if the Word has fallen onto hard ground, if it gets choked out, or if it is snatched away before it can grow, that person will likely deconstruct whatever faith they had.

Then there is the matter of the nature of truth. If people do not understand that there is objective truth—or if they don't put Christianity in that category—they are more likely to deconstruct. That's why both our vocabulary and the use of logic in our thought processes matter so much.

LEADER'S NOTE

Your main goal this week is to help people delve deeper into the anatomy of deconstruction. Participants should come away with a better understanding of where deconstructors are coming from, as well as increased compassion for their pain that can translate into hope and help for those who are struggling.

READ

Before your meeting, read chapters 5 and 6 ("Crisis" and "Upper Story") in *The Deconstruction of Christianity*.

WATCH VIDEO SESSION 3

In this video, Alisa and Tim share some of their personal stories and discuss the trigger events and ideologies that cause some people to deconstruct.

- What are some of the factors that affect whether someone deconverts or reconstructs their faith after a crisis?

- What is the difference between "upper-story" and "lower-story" truth?

- What are some statements that belong in the upper story, and what are some statements that belong in the lower story?

DISCUSS

1. The action step from last week was to stay calm as you think about and interact with someone who is deconstructing their faith. How did you bring your own fears and doubts to the Lord this week? What Scriptures encouraged you?

Let's start at the beginning of the deconstruction journey. The main difference between someone who deconstructs and someone who remains in the faith is the foundation they begin with.

> "Listen! A farmer went out to plant some seed. As he scattered it across his field, some of the seed fell on a footpath, and the birds came and ate it. Other seed fell on shallow soil with underlying rock. The seed sprouted quickly because the soil was shallow. But the plant soon wilted under the hot sun, and since it didn't have deep roots, it died. Other seed fell among thorns that grew up and choked out the tender plants so they produced no grain. Still other seeds fell on fertile soil, and they sprouted, grew, and produced a crop that was thirty, sixty, and even a hundred times as much as had been planted!"

Then [Jesus] said, "Anyone with ears to hear should listen and understand."

Later, when Jesus was alone with the twelve disciples and with the others who were gathered around, they asked him what the parables meant.

He replied, "You are permitted to understand the secret of the Kingdom of God. But I use parables for everything I say to outsiders, so that the Scriptures might be fulfilled:

'When they see what I do,
    they will learn nothing.
When they hear what I say,
    they will not understand.
Otherwise, they will turn to me
    and be forgiven.'"

Then Jesus said to them, "If you can't understand the meaning of this parable, how will you understand all the other parables? The farmer plants seed by taking God's word to others. The seed that fell on the footpath represents those who hear the message, only to have Satan come at once and take it away. The seed on the rocky soil represents those who hear the message and immediately receive it with joy. But since they don't have deep roots, they don't last long. They fall away as soon as they have problems or are persecuted for believing God's word. The seed that fell among the thorns represents others who hear God's word, but all too quickly the message is crowded out by the worries of this life, the lure of

wealth, and the desire for other things, so no fruit
is produced. And the seed that fell on good soil
represents those who hear and accept God's word and
produce a harvest of thirty, sixty, or even a hundred
times as much as had been planted!"

MARK 4:3-20

2. Fill out the chart below based on Mark 4:3-20.

TYPE OF SOIL	TYPE OF GROWTH	FINAL RESULT	SPIRITUAL TRUTH

3. Which of these types of soil do you think most often
   create the right environment for deconstruction?

Each person's faith foundation is constructed from an almost endless list of unique variables. And as with an earthquake, the crisis can vary between types of movement (earthquakes can quake up and down or side to side), its magnitude (which relates to the size of the fault line), and so on. These variables together will impact how much damage is done. This is why each deconstruction is unique. Each person's spiritual foundation, from base to roof, is different. That foundation intersects with different types of crises, with several sometimes appearing at once.

The Deconstruction of Christianity, pages 82–83

4. Along with all the variables in a person's spiritual foundation, there are also various triggers that can lead to deconstruction. Place a check mark next to the ones that have been part of your faith journey. For each of the triggers listed, discuss what you think might help someone who is struggling with that particular issue to keep their faith. If someone faces this crisis, how might you help them overcome it? What are some Bible passages that speak to each issue?

☐ Suffering

☐ Doubt

☐ Politics

☐ Purity culture

☐ Questions about the Bible

☐ Morality/toxic theology

☐ Abuse

While the triggers described in [chapter 5] might be valid reasons to become confused about what Christianity is and cause someone to wrestle with the nature of God along with the truthfulness of certain teachings and doctrines, none of them is a good reason to leave the historic faith or redefine it according to one's subjective preferences.

The Deconstruction of Christianity, page 98

It's easy to understand why these triggers might lead someone to deconstruct, and that helps us have compassion for people whose faith struggles are set off by these events. But that is, of course, only part of the picture. Somehow they move from a crisis into full-blown faith deconstruction, a result of how they are defining truth and where they are going for answers to their questions.

In order to disentangle the confusion and lies that lead to deconstruction, we need to define what people mean by "truth" and understand what kinds of things they put in that category.

Correspondence theory of truth: A statement is true if it corresponds with reality. This assumes that there is *objective truth*, in which a person's belief or preferences are irrelevant to the truth of a statement. The "truth maker" lies outside the individual.

Subjective truth or relativism: What is true or false depends on the individual—the subject. The "truth maker" is the individual's tastes, preferences, or beliefs.

5. Explain in your own words why relativism is self-defeating. What is the logical flaw in the idea that "what is true for me may not be true for you"?

6. In the house below, the bottom story is for public, provable facts about reality, and the top story is for personal belief statements. Write several truth statements in the drawing, placing each on the appropriate level. Then compare answers with your group to see if you agree on where each should go.

PERSONAL BELIEFS/SUBJECTIVE TRUTH CLAIMS

FACTS ABOUT REALITY/OBJECTIVE TRUTH

7. According to the culture at large, where would the statement "Christianity is true" go in this diagram? What are the practical consequences of putting faith in this category?

When we say, "Christianity is true," there's a common confusion that occurs. Our contemporary culture thinks we're claiming, "Christianity is true for me." They assume we're making a subjective claim, not an objective one. . . . But we're not merely claiming that Christianity is our personal preference. We're claiming that Christianity is true to reality—it fits the way the world really is. It's objectively true.

The Deconstruction of Christianity, pages 105–106

8. In personal relationships or public discourse, what are the consequences of misunderstanding the type of truth claim we are making when we say, "Christianity is true"?

Then Jesus said to his disciples, "If any of you wants to be my follower, you must give up your own way, take up your cross, and follow me."

MATTHEW 16:24

9. In view of Jesus' words in Matthew 16:24, what sacrifices or life choices have you made that are appropriate because Christianity can hold up under exacting rational examination and also satisfy our highest spiritual aspirations?

The claim of Jesus' deity is important because if it's not true, then Jesus was just "living his truth." That would actually make him a liar or a lunatic for claiming to be God, as C. S. Lewis famously pointed out.[6] However, if his assertion is true, then it's true to reality.

This is one of the reasons the resurrection of Jesus is such a bedrock teaching. The Resurrection is a fact about reality—an objective truth—that isn't just true for those who believe it. Jesus was either raised from the dead, as a historical event in reality, or he wasn't. If he wasn't, then Christianity is false. If he was, then Christianity is true for everyone, whether they believe it or not. Because of that, it has eternal consequences for everyone. . . .

If Christianity is true, it makes exclusive claims about itself. Jesus claimed, "I am the way, and the truth, and the life. No one comes to the Father except through me" (John 14:6). He predicted his own death and resurrection (John 2:19; 10:18), and then he proved his claims true by raising himself from the dead.

The Deconstruction of Christianity, pages 107–108

10. Why is it hypocritical or illogical for a deconstructionist to claim they are nonjudgmental? What beliefs do they seem to consider heretical?

Deconstruction is a flawed process. It assigns religious belief to the upper story, treating truth as a matter of personal preference, and makes the individual the ultimate authority.

The Deconstruction of Christianity, page 117

In addition to trying to understand someone else's story, we need to come to terms with our own. On an emotional level, part of being a healthy person is simply facing up to our struggles. Beyond that, understanding why we have held on to our faith through adversity and other threats gives us a common ground with those who are deconstructing. We don't want to approach these things with a judgmental attitude or act as if our story is more important than someone else's, but we do want to see where our stories intersect so we can come alongside them as a friend.

11. If you call yourself a Christian, why are you a Christian? What arguments and experiences played a role in your Christian conversion?

12. What challenges to your faith have you faced and overcome?

13. Thinking about specific people you know who are deconstructing or personal testimonies you have encountered, what are some practical things Christians can do to help others understand the ideas presented in these chapters? What are some of the most compelling arguments for the objective truth of Christianity, and how can they be made winsomely?

Christianity is not merely subjective truth; it is true truth. . . . It is truth that explains reality.

The Deconstruction of Christianity, page 108

PRAY

Close your time together with prayer. Invite group members to share how they are grappling with the ideas inherent in deconstruction. Also share about any interactions group members have had with their struggling friends since your last meeting. Keep praying for the list of family members and friends as you and your group work to understand the deconstructionist movement. End with a simple prayer such as the one below:

> *Dear heavenly Father,*
>
> *Thank you for revealing truth to us. Thank you that you can be known and that you love us. Help us to understand and believe the truth so that we can have life in your name. Help us to build a strong foundation and grow our roots deep into you so that when crises and faith struggles come, we will remain firm and steadfast. Guide us as we interact with people who are deconstructing. May we be bold and winsome in our witness for you. Amen.*

REFLECT

Before the next group meeting, take some time to reflect on what was discussed this week and how to put it into practice.

- Are there areas where your faith foundation is not as firm as it should be? Where could you learn more or find support for that particular struggle?

• Have you experienced crises or trigger points that you have not fully processed? How could you deal with those?

• Pay attention this week to the times you see people place religion in the realm of upper-story truth only. What patterns do you see?

• Are you prepared to respond to those who assume Christianity is merely a matter of personal preference? If not, how could you expand your understanding of the issues?

TAKE ACTION

Keep praying for those who are deconstructing, stay calm, and add this week's action step: **Stay in their lives.** With so much at stake and so much personal concern, it is tempting to want to pull back when relationships get difficult. That's the last thing we should do. When someone is struggling in their faith, that's the time to draw close to them in love. It can also be tempting to try to fix their theology in a quick meeting. If the relationship allows, ask questions to help them process their faith, and don't be afraid of their questions even if you don't have good answers for them yet. Use this time to establish the relationship without bringing up spiritual matters. Here are some ways you can connect.

- Do something to make your friend or family member feel loved without pushing too hard.
- Hang out (go for lunch, grab a coffee, or see a movie) without bringing up Christianity or their deconstruction. Just spend time together. (Yes, it's okay to do that.)
- Shoot them a quick text to let them know that you love them and are there for them no matter where they land theologically.

PREPARE

Session 4 covers chapters 7 and 8 ("Reformation" and "Toxic") in *The Deconstruction of Christianity*. Read those chapters in preparation for your next meeting. As you read, think about these questions:

- Is deconstruction really a form of reformation that seeks to root out falsehood and abuses from the church?

- What do people mean by the phrase *toxic theology*?

HOW ARE THEY DECONSTRUCTING?

Responding to Claims of "Toxic" Theology

Now that we understand some of the reasons why people deconstruct, we turn to the *how* question: What is the process? How are they deconstructing? The short answer is that deconstructors are challenging whatever they deem to be "toxic." Granted, there are false beliefs that need to be corrected and abuses that need to be called out. But the solution is reformation, not deconstruction. We want to reform our beliefs and behavior according to Scripture. This is what Martin Luther modeled for us, and it's what every Christian should be engaged in as they follow Jesus. That's not what deconstructors are doing—they aren't going through a process of reforming to be more faithful to God's Word; they are rejecting God's Word.

As we make clear in *The Deconstruction of Christianity*, we don't want Christians to disengage their minds or to blindly accept the teachings of a particular pastor or thinker. We aren't advocating for an unexamined faith or for the absence of questions. What we want Christians to do is remind ourselves why the Bible is a reliable authority for faith and life, and then to reform our faith back to what the Bible teaches us about God and ourselves. We want to reconstruct our faith by asking questions in search of answers and then aligning our lives according to the truth.

LEADER'S NOTE

Your main goals this week are to encourage healthy questions that lead to faith reformation and to disarm the notion that Christianity is toxic. If some group participants feel they have been attacked by people claiming that our faith is dangerous, be aware that the discussion could veer off topic more easily this week. You want to walk the line between helping group members with the real-life situations they are encountering and keeping the discussion on track.

READ

Before your meeting, read chapters 7 and 8 ("Reformation" and "Toxic") in *The Deconstruction of Christianity*.

WATCH VIDEO SESSION 4

In this video, Alisa and Tim discuss why deconstruction is not the same as reconstruction and what is meant by toxic theology. As you watch the video, jot down a few notes.

- What are the assumptions and ideas behind the phrase *toxic theology*?

- How is deconstruction different from reformation?

- Was there ever a time when a statement you made turned into a conversation about toxicity rather than truth?

DISCUSS

1. What is one part of the Bible you have had trouble coming to terms with, or an unanswered question you have about the Bible?

Some deconstructionists claim that they are merely reconstructing or reforming their faith. But the word *reconstruction* implies that you are going back to the origin of something—in this case, Christian faith. And by definition, reconstruction has to be based on an objective standard, which is the Bible. That isn't what deconstructionists are doing. Many base their beliefs on their own opinions or on popular cultural beliefs. And more often than not, they are headed away from the Christian faith they began with.

2. What is your reaction to using the term *reformation* in relation to faith? Do you agree or disagree with the idea that the opposite of deconstruction isn't shutting down all questions but rather asking them with a different basis and a different goal? Why did you answer the way you did?

The unexamined faith is not worth believing. An examined faith is a healthy faith. That's why it's important that we examine and reexamine our beliefs. Every Christian should know what they believe and why they believe it. And this means being open to asking hard questions.

The Deconstruction of Christianity, page 120

The people of Berea were more open-minded than those in Thessalonica, and they listened eagerly to Paul's message. They searched the Scriptures day after day to see if Paul and Silas were teaching the truth.

ACTS 17:11

3. What does Acts 17:11 tell us about the right response to a new teaching or a new idea? What makes the difference between the reformation of an individual's faith and its deconstruction?

One of the common defenses that many deconstructionists make on social media—and a tactic they use to get others to join their cause—is that they are asking questions that no one else is brave enough to ask. In reality, they are usually simply trying to find an escape hatch. Unlike the reformers of old, who were returning to Scripture and trying to form their lives around it, the prophets of deconstruction begin their crusade by attacking the Bible. Once the authority of Scripture is dethroned, the authority of self is crowned in its place.

When Christians find themselves struggling with questions about their faith, a better practice is reformation, *not deconstruction. . . . Reformation is the process of correcting mistaken beliefs* to make them align with Scripture.

The Deconstruction of Christianity, page 125

4. According to chapter 7 or your own additional research, what good reasons do we have to believe the Bible is true? Simplify the argument down to the way you would answer someone who asked, "Why do you believe the Bible?"

After dethroning the authority of Scripture, step two on the deconstruction journey is to attack what most deconstructionists call "toxic theology." This can be any doctrine they deem to be outdated or opposed to their preferred belief system. Simply by calling it toxic and characterizing it in a negative light, they are able to cast doubt on every related belief as well.

From the perspective of deconstructionists, there is no false theology to be corrected. There is only "toxic" theology to be deconstructed. Toxic theology is a catchall term being used to describe any doctrine one deems harmful.

The Deconstruction of Christianity, page 139

5. What are some examples of theological beliefs you have heard referred to as toxic?

6. Choose one of those "toxic" beliefs and explain what the deconstructionist is assuming about Christianity that isn't true.

7. As you think about the way some deconstructionists frame that same "toxic" belief, what would you say are the motives they assign to Christianity?

> To refer to original sin as "toxic" makes sense only if it's not true.
> If it is true, the gospel is the cure.
>
> The Deconstruction of Christianity, page 140

8. How would you go about convincing someone that the Christian belief you chose to consider in item 6 is not actually toxic? What arguments might you use?

Critical theory is one ideology that deconstructionists use to redefine Christian beliefs as "toxic." It has gained popularity in recent years to the point where this belief system has pervaded everything from political debates to discussions of gender rights. But what exactly is critical theory, and how is it being used by deconstructionists?

Critical theory functions like a worldview that understands and critiques power and oppression along the lines of race, ethnicity, class, gender, ability, sexuality, and other factors. It primarily sees the world through the lens of oppressed groups and their oppressors and attempts to recalibrate power in favor of the marginalized [thus making] the false assumption that original sin is about keeping people under the church's power.

The Deconstruction of Christianity, pages 142–143

This creates specific patterns of thought that work like a contagion to cast doubt on truth and lead to hostility toward Christians.

Here's how the deconstruction project works in three simple steps.

Step one: *Identify a problem in society.*

Step two: *Show how the church actively endorsed or passively allowed injustice.*

Step three: *Conclude that "hundreds of years of participation in white supremacy, patriarchy, and nationalism have warped 'white evangelical theology' such that it needs to be fundamentally reimagined."[7] . . .*

When examining evangelical positions, the primary question for these writers isn't "Is the belief true?" or even "What does the Bible teach?" but "Has this belief been used to oppress?" . . . This form of deconstruction is about undermining perceived oppression, not falsifying truth claims.

The Deconstruction of Christianity, pages 145–146

9. How do you see critical theory at work in the thought processes of those you know who are deconstructing? Trace the three steps they are using to deconstruct a particular theological belief, such as the doctrine of original sin, hell, or penal substitutionary atonement.

10. How might you attempt to show a deconstructionist the inherent problems in this thought process? How are they being illogical and unfair to Christianity when they frame theological tenets of the faith in terms of critical theory?

The desire to unravel any Christian doctrines that have become wrapped up in unrelated cultural mores is a good one. We do want to distill our beliefs down to what the Bible actually says and how it applies to our lives. And of course we are against abuse, and we want to root it out of our churches. But the way to do that is not to reframe everything as abuser vs. victim. That is simply a new form of false teaching like the ones Paul warned us about.

As Christians, we should seek to reject false ideas. We ought to stand against abuse. But we will be unable to discern whether or not a teaching is abusive if we don't have a way to know what is correct in the first place. And we certainly cannot settle these theological disputes without an objective standard to appeal to. This requires the Bible. Deciding theological positions by what one perceives to be helpful vs. harmful, oppressive vs. liberating, or right vs. wrong is an invalid method for doing theology.

The Deconstruction of Christianity, page 150

11. Read Paul's description of the dangers of false apostles in 2 Corinthians 11:3-4, 13-15.

I fear that somehow your pure and undivided devotion to Christ will be corrupted, just as Eve was deceived by the cunning ways of the serpent. You happily put up with whatever anyone tells you, even if they preach a different Jesus than the one we preach, or a different kind of Spirit than the one you received, or a different kind of gospel than the one you believed. . . .

These people are false apostles. They are deceitful workers who disguise themselves as apostles of Christ. But I am not surprised! Even Satan disguises himself as an angel of light. So it is no wonder that his servants also disguise themselves as servants of righteousness. In the end they will get the punishment their wicked deeds deserve.

2 CORINTHIANS 11:3-4, 13-15

What does Paul say about these false teachers' . . .

a. character

b. motives

c. strategies

12. What is the effect of these false teachings on the church?

13. How does this match up with your experience of
    deconstructionists in the church, such as those
    described in this week's chapters? Where do you see
    deconstructionists in this description of false apostles?
    How are today's deconstructionists different from the
    false apostles of Paul's day?

*It's one thing to claim that a person can have a false view of
God. It's entirely another to propose that false views of God
have been affirmed by the Bible. The Bible is the standard by
which we determine if our view of God is correct or faulty. But
a [postmodern] sleight of hand could lead someone to conclude
that even the very Word of God is something that calls for a bit
of deconstruction.*

The Deconstruction of Christianity, page 156

14. What is one theological position that you have
    studied to satisfy your own curiosity or answer your
    own questions? How did you go about gathering
    information about that topic?

PRAY

Close your time together with prayer. Invite group members
to share their progress in engaging with deconstruction and
then uphold one another in prayer. Keep praying for the list
of family members and friends as group members learn more
about the deconstructionist movement. End with a simple
prayer such as the one below:

Dear heavenly Father,

*Thank you for holding us close even as we ask questions
and struggle with our faith. Help us to be honest with
our questions and wise in seeking answers. We long to
know you better. Help us to see you more clearly even
as we consider the ways culture is attacking our faith.
Thank you that you are holy and just, and that your
love is unfailing and never-ending. Most of all, thank
you for promising that when we ask you for wisdom*

*and pray for answers, you will reveal yourself to us
and show us how to answer those who attack the faith.
Amen.*

REFLECT

Before the next group meeting, take some time to reflect on
what was discussed this week and how to put it into practice.

- Do you have reliable resources or trusted individuals
  you can turn to when you have questions or doubts
  about your faith? What could you do to gather a list
  of trustworthy resources?

- What is one theological issue you want to study in
  greater depth? How can you gather information in a
  way that is intellectually and theologically responsible?

- Take some extended time this week to pray and read your Bible. Take to heart the promise of Matthew 7:7-11 below and be persistent in seeking answers.

> Keep on asking, and you will receive what you ask for. Keep on seeking, and you will find. Keep on knocking, and the door will be opened to you. For everyone who asks, receives. Everyone who seeks, finds. And to everyone who knocks, the door will be opened.
> You parents—if your children ask for a loaf of bread, do you give them a stone instead? Or if they ask for a fish, do you give them a snake? Of course not! So if you sinful people know how to give good gifts to your children, how much more will your heavenly Father give good gifts to those who ask him.
>
> MATTHEW 7:7-11

TAKE ACTION

As you've interacted with your friend or loved one who is deconstructing their faith, you've undoubtedly come across some questions you can't answer right away. That's why this week's action step is to do some **triage**. Get out your journal and write down specifically what their struggles and questions are, and then look for answers you can share with them. As you do, take care of yourself—remember that someone else's deconstruction can feel like a death or a divorce as they walk away from the faith you once shared.

PREPARE

Session 5 covers chapters 9 and 10 ("Faith" and "Deconstructor") in *The Deconstruction of Christianity*. Read those chapters in preparation for your next meeting. As you read, think about these questions:

- What is the difference between "the faith" and "my faith," and why does it matter?

- Why is it important to understand faith as a relationship?

WHAT IS BEING DECONSTRUCTED?

Separating the Christian Faith from Personal Opinions

Once we grasp the process of deconstruction, we need to examine the *what* behind it. What is being deconstructed? This is where there is a lot of confusion about what Christianity actually *is*—and *is not*. We're going to sort that out this week.

It begins with understanding the nature of faith. When someone talks about their faith, they mean either the historical tenets of Christianity (the faith), their personal relationship or non-relationship with God (personal faith), or both. And we need to know which it is in any given conversation.

Then we need to see how faith intersects with real-life struggles and how that can lead people to deconstruct. We are humans made in the image of God, made for a "very good" world where we can live in a relationship with him.

But we now live in a fallen world. Things are not as they should be, either in our hearts or in the places we inhabit. We are sinners, separated from the one who made us and loves us. When we search for truth, there are obstacles to belief that must be overcome. These challenges lead us either toward God or away from him. These struggles lead us either into the arms of Jesus or into the self-destructive path of disbelief and deconstruction.

It's only after we have an accurate understanding of who we are as humans that we can begin to make sense of where our deconstructing loved ones are coming from.

LEADER'S NOTE

Your main goal this week is to help participants distinguish between their own faith, which may include extrabiblical or even incorrect assumptions, and the historic Christian faith, whose unchanging tenets are revealed in Scripture. You'll want to create an atmosphere of gentle humility that seeks to listen compassionately and discern the heart's cry of each person in your group. This week's discussion may bring up some powerful emotions, and that's okay. For many people in the group, this may be the first time they've been able to share their heart for those they love who are deconstructing.

READ

Before your meeting, read chapters 9 and 10 ("Faith" and "Deconstructor") in *The Deconstruction of Christianity*.

WATCH VIDEO SESSION 5

In this video, Alisa and Tim discuss what is being deconstructed: faith. They identify important distinctions between *your* faith and *the* Christian faith that was "once for all delivered to the saints" (Jude 1:3, esv). As you watch the video, jot down a few notes.

- Why is it important for you to understand *what* is being deconstructed?

- How does viewing faith as a relationship, not merely a set of beliefs, help you better understand what your loved one is going through?

- How do *the* Christian faith and *your* Christian faith relate to each other? What does it mean to have true faith in Jesus?

DISCUSS

1. This is session 5 of our study together. What has surprised you? What new insights have you gained about your own faith and the deconstruction movement?

2. In your conversations with others, do you speak more often about "the faith" or "my/your faith"? Why is the difference between them important in our conversations with deconstructors?

The distinction between the faith—historic Christian beliefs—and an individual believer's personal faith relationship with God is important in this discussion because it helps us understand why these issues run so deep. Faith matters to us because it's not merely upper-story preferences; it is emphatically a lower-story truth. If what the Bible claims is true, it changes everything about our lives. And that's the real issue many deconstructionists are facing. They don't like the implications of Christianity. That's also why we as Christians care enough to engage with these issues. This matters more than anything else in our lives.

Paul has no trouble telling [Galatian] Christians what their faith needs to look like because he is working from a different understanding of faith. For Paul, your *faith can't be whatever you want it to be. Your faith needs to match up with* the *faith—what Paul takes to be objective reality.*

The Deconstruction of Christianity, pages 160–161

3. When it comes to faith, what is the difference between "believing that" and "believing in"?

The Christian faith stands independent of any individual. It's like gravity, an objective feature of the world. Someone can deny gravity exists, yet he will fall to the ground if he jumps from the top of a building, no matter how strongly he believes he can fly.

The Deconstruction of Christianity, page 163

4. What happens if someone only "believes that" without also "trusting in" Jesus? What are the results of having only an objective faith without the subjective element?

When someone is going through faith deconstruction, it's important to understand what they mean by faith—that is, the precise beliefs they are deconstructing—so we know exactly what it is that they're rejecting. After all, many people have a personal faith (that is, a belief system) that doesn't match an accurate "once for all delivered to the saints" faith. . . . Often in the deconstruction explosion, people mistake their own personal faith, which might be full of incorrect beliefs, with the authentic Christian faith.

The Deconstruction of Christianity, page 163

As we grow in our faith, we will discover that there are some parts of our understanding that are not part of the faith— parts of our cultural Christian experience that turn out to be merely preferences or even misunderstandings of Scripture. Maturity involves understanding the difference between biblical truth and extrabiblical religiosity—and rejecting the latter. This isn't deconstruction; it's reforming true faith.

5. From what you've observed, what are some common incorrect beliefs people deconstruct? What is the result of disentangling these false beliefs that are not part of the faith "once for all delivered to the saints"?

6. What are some beliefs you used to accept uncritically but have now rejected based on new information or a deeper understanding of Scripture? How has rejecting those incorrect beliefs affected you? (These don't necessarily need to be big spiritual truths; the example in the book was about a spider!)

Christianity isn't merely a commitment to a set of propositions. It's a commitment to a person. *Often, faith is treated as a set of propositions that can be dissected, examined, accepted, and, if need be, rejected. Of course, Christianity entails a set of beliefs, but it's more than that. It's a relationship with a person—Jesus.*

The Deconstruction of Christianity, pages 165–166

7. How might thinking of unpacking deconstruction as *vivisection* of a living entity, rather than *dissection* of something that is already dead change how you interact with someone who is deconstructing?

Read John 1:10-18.

He came into the very world he created, but
the world didn't recognize him. He came to his
own people, and even they rejected him. But to
all who believed him and accepted him, he gave
the right to become children of God. They are
reborn—not with a physical birth resulting from
human passion or plan, but a birth that comes
from God.

So the Word became human and made his
home among us. He was full of unfailing love and
faithfulness. And we have seen his glory, the glory
of the Father's one and only Son.

John testified about him when he shouted
to the crowds, "This is the one I was talking
about when I said, 'Someone is coming after me
who is far greater than I am, for he existed long
before me.'"

From his abundance we have all received one
gracious blessing after another. For the law was
given through Moses, but God's unfailing love
and faithfulness came through Jesus Christ. No
one has ever seen God. But the unique One, who
is himself God, is near to the Father's heart. He
has revealed God to us.

JOHN 1:10-18

8. Based on these verses, how would you characterize a believer's relationship with God and God's disposition toward us?

9. Based on these verses, how would you describe the effects of leaving the Christian faith on

   a. the individual who is deconstructing?

   b. Christians who are watching it happen?

Deconstructing faith is not just about dismantling particular beliefs and deciding to reject them or trade one worldview for another. The consequences mirror what might happen if someone were to rethink what they believed about their marriage, a scenario that would involve deeply felt consequences that would impact their spousal relationship.

The Deconstruction of Christianity, page 167

10. How might thinking of the Christian faith as a personal relationship rather than as a set of beliefs change the way you interact with someone who is deconstructing? How can this help you better know how to influence their journey?

One of the reasons people are quick to deconstruct is because they view faith as belief in the absence of evidence. But that isn't what the Christian faith is at all. It's not a blind leap into the dark. Rather, it's a step of trust in what we have reason to believe is true. *The* faith becomes *our* faith because it explains reality in a way that makes sense. Let's consider some of the reasons we believe.

11. What are some of the evidences for the Christian faith that have been most convincing to you?

12. How has your faith affected your life? What evidence of active faith would others see in you?

Every deconstructor, even the most hardened and angry, has a very personal story about how they got to the point of deconstruction. Often these stories are painful, and understanding them will help us know what is really going on in their heart and how we might be able to help.

13. What are some questions or tactics you have found helpful in uncovering what's really behind someone's deconstruction story?

14. How does it help us better deal with deconstructors to understand that we are all made in the image of God? How should that affect the way we speak and the things we say to them?

15. How should the truth that all of us are sinners affect our understanding of deconstructors and the way we interact with them?

Most people are quite comfortable living in sin. And we certainly don't like being judged for it. But that's precisely the problem. A sinner searching for God is like a fugitive searching for the police. Many don't want to find him.

The Deconstruction of Christianity, page 185

Humans are by nature seekers, though not everyone who says they are seeking truth is actually doing so. Sometimes they are seeking followers or self-satisfaction or escape from their pain. Understanding the desires and goals of a deconstructor can help us better respond to their questions and arguments.

16. What do you think the deconstructors you know are seeking? How might answering that question for an individual deconstructor affect how you interact with them?

There's a temptation to think that if we could just provide enough evidence, people would believe. It's as if people have an "evidence meter" in their heads, and when the device reaches a certain level, they believe in God. But this assumes that everyone is on an earnest truth quest, and it's not that simple. In reality, the heart behind people's seeking will play an important role in whether or not they discover truth. . . . The problem is not with God's failure to give evidence; the problem is with our failure to accept it.

The Deconstruction of Christianity, pages 188–189

But now you are free from the power of sin and have become slaves of God. Now you do those things that lead to holiness and result in eternal life.

ROMANS 6:22

17. One thing deconstructors seek and seem to find is a type of freedom. How does Romans 6:22 define true freedom, and how might you help others find it?

18. What is one takeaway from this week's discussion that you will put into practice before our next meeting (e.g., one new way of understanding deconstructors that will change how you interact with them)?

PRAY

Close your time together with prayer. Invite group members to share briefly about their struggles, particularly as they pertain to deconstruction. Pray again for the list of family members and friends whom group members are praying for as they work to understand faith deconstruction. Close with a simple prayer such as the one below:

Dear heavenly Father,

Thank you that you can breathe new life even into dead bones. Sometimes our faith feels dry and fragile, and the faith of those we love can seem even more so. Help us to turn to you, the only source of truth and life, with our struggles and doubts. Enliven our hearts so we can see you more clearly and trust you with our lives. Help us to listen well and have the eyes of our hearts opened so we can gently and winsomely speak truth to those who are in danger of falling away. Give us the gift of discernment and the ability to respond to others with loving humility. Amen.

REFLECT

Before the next group meeting, take some time to reflect on what was discussed this week and how to put it into practice.

- What are some ideas and strategies you want to pull from this week's discussion as you interact with people who are deconstructing their faith? What can you apply to the issues you are dealing with right now?

- What do you think may be influencing the people you know who are deconstructing? The answers likely lie in their motives, desires, and experiences.

> This is what the Sovereign LORD says: Look! I
> am going to put breath into you and make you
> live again! I will put flesh and muscles on you
> and cover you with skin. I will put breath into
> you, and you will come to life. Then you will
> know that I am the LORD.
>
> EZEKIEL 37:5-6

- Look up and meditate on the larger passage in Ezekiel 37:1-14 as you pray that those whose faith is dead will find eternal life by the Spirit of God.

TAKE ACTION

This week probably brought up some things for you— feelings you didn't realize ran as deep as they do or new ways of approaching your friends who are deconstructing. That brings us to this week's action step: **Set some boundaries.**

Maybe you need to set some boundaries so you aren't negatively affected by watching someone you love struggle. Perhaps you need to set some boundaries around your relationship so you can continue to be a good friend without constantly bombarding them with questions and arguments.

We'll talk more about this in session 6, but for now, begin asking yourself what boundaries you need to put in place to protect you, your loved one, and your relationship.

PREPARE

Session 6 covers chapters 11–13 ("Questions," "Advice," and "Saturday") in *The Deconstruction of Christianity*. Read those chapters in preparation for your next meeting. As you read, think about these questions:

- Does my church make room for people to ask questions?

- Through this study, how have I grown in my ability to come alongside someone who is deconstructing? In what areas do I need to grow?

WHERE DO WE GO FROM HERE?

Working toward Reformation

We've said it before and we'll keep on saying it: Asking questions can be a very good thing for our faith. If we didn't ask questions such as *How did I get here?* and *Why am I here?* we wouldn't ever seek God. We also wouldn't really have much reason to get up in the morning. And if we didn't reexamine the answers we were given as children to these types of questions, we wouldn't grow into mature faith. Asking questions and finding answers are part of seeking God, and we won't find him if we don't seek him.

Curiosity helps us uncover the truth. It leads us to a deeper relationship with God, one where we feel free to be honest—and thus more intimate with him. And it helps us engage with the world in a new way. From the first "why" questions of a toddler to the end of life, we should all be asking questions every day of our lives.

Of course, there are some potential problems with the way most deconstructors are asking their questions and the outcome they are working toward. They tend to ask questions that assume that Christians and the God of the Bible have bad motives. But the questions themselves aren't bad. In fact, even questions asked with a good deal of skepticism can lead to truth-finding.

And that's where we hope you will go with your deconstructing friends. Listen to their questions. Uncover the assumptions, misinformation, and hurts that might be behind the questions. If it's an honest question, do your best to address it without pushing too hard.

This session is designed to help you process everything you've been discussing for the past five sessions and come up with an action plan for how you will interact with the people in your world who are deconstructing. Whether it's online, in a coffee shop, or in your own home, we hope you'll keep engaging with the questions people are asking and the people who are asking them.

LEADER'S NOTE

Your main goals this week are to summarize lessons learned and help participants create an action plan for what to do with the things they've been learning. Many of these questions are process oriented and may need to be considered at more length after your group time, but raising them in a group setting will help participants get on the right track. At the end of your time together, you might want to schedule a follow-up session in a few weeks to see how people are doing and discuss any questions or insights that have come up as people continue to wrestle with these topics. In addition, be sure to stress the importance of doing the reflection questions at the end of this session. Participants will need to do those at home even if you're not meeting again.

READ

Before your meeting, read chapters 11–13 ("Questions," "Advice," and "Saturday") in *The Deconstruction of Christianity*.

WATCH VIDEO SESSION 6

In this video, Alisa and Tim offer hope and help for the deconstructors and those who love them. As you watch the video, jot down a few notes.

- What should our first response be when we interact with those who are deconstructing?

- What are some possible takeaways or action steps God might be prompting you to pursue?

• Where do you see hope? Where do you see God at work? What gives you hope?

DISCUSS

1. As you think back on your group time and the book *The Deconstruction of Christianity*, are you more hopeful about the future of those who are deconstructing their faith than you were when you began? Or are you now more concerned about the effects of deconstructionism on the church and in culture? Explain your answer.

2. The introductory section of part 3 in the book describes the experience of Dave Stovall, who deconstructed his faith and then reconstructed it. Look back at his story on pages 199–201 and jot down some reasons you think he was able to reconstruct. What can you take

away from his story and put into practice in your own relationships and your own church?

One of the reasons the church hasn't dealt very successfully with the deconstruction movement is that we haven't always provided an opportunity for people to ask questions. There are some valid reasons for that. As we try to communicate truth and persuade people that Scripture has the answers they seek, some may get the impression that it's wrong to ask questions about the Bible.

In addition, finding the right venue for asking and answering questions requires some creativity, since it isn't part of the traditional church format. At times, people with questions don't ask them in church for fear others might perceive these questions as threatening. But we must remember that God isn't threatened by our queries. In fact, he welcomes them.

3. Have you found your church to be a welcome place to ask questions? Explain your answer.

4. What do you think happens when we bury our questions rather than asking them and seeking answers?

Strictly speaking, doubts and questions are not *the problem. In fact, when honest doubts are carefully explored, this can lead to strong faith formation. However, when doubts are carelessly ignored or suppressed, this can lead to faith destruction. Sadly, this is what the online world is witnessing in the deconstruction movement.*

The Deconstruction of Christianity, page 209

5. What are some of the challenges churches face in making space for questions?

6. What practical solutions can you think of for overcoming these challenges?

7. What are some potential dangers of a church focusing too much on asking and answering questions? How could making space for questions be done in a healthy, balanced way?

Providing opportunities for people to express doubt and ask questions is a start, but it's not where we want to end. We want to address the questions that have good answers in the Bible and accept where the Bible expresses mystery and simply doesn't give us answers.

8. When you have asked questions in church or about your faith, have you received satisfying answers? What do you think are the general characteristics of a good answer to an honest faith question?

Thoughtful questions demand thoughtful answers. When we respond with half-baked or pat answers, we communicate that we're not taking the questions seriously—or even worse, that we simply don't have any good answers. Bad answers shut down sincere questions.

The Deconstruction of Christianity, page 209

9. What are some characteristics of a bad response to an honest faith question?

10. How can we help our churches offer better answers, even to difficult questions? What are some ways we might hold churches or Christian thought leaders accountable for listening and answering well?

We can offer space for questions and provide good answers to honest questions, but they might not be accepted. Not everyone is truly seeking answers, and even those who are might not be ready to respond in faith. Though we wish it were otherwise, we can't control the outcome of a conversation or an invitation to faith—only God can do that.

When asked difficult questions, church leaders are sometimes quite well-equipped to answer them, but the answers they give aren't ones the questioner wants to hear. It's not that the answers aren't true; it's that the answers aren't accepted.

The Deconstruction of Christianity, page 214

11. What should we do when we offer a good answer to a deconstructionist's question but they just won't accept it?

For Christians who are made in the image of God, the desire to know is God-given. We were created to question. In fact, God asks questions. This is odd if you think about it. Why would an all-knowing God ask questions? It can't be because he doesn't know something. That answer won't work. When God asks questions, it's not for his benefit; it's for ours.

The Deconstruction of Christianity, pages 216–217

12. What are some questions God asks of people in the Bible? (Here are a few to take a look at: Genesis 3:9, 13; 16:8; Exodus 4:2; 1 Kings 19:9; Job 38:4; Isaiah 6:8; Jonah 4:4; Ezekiel 37:3; Matthew 20:32.) What do these tell you about how God interacts with people? What do they imply about how you should interact with people?

Virtually every deconstruction testimony talks about "unanswered questions." That's part of the story . . . but it's not the whole story. That's because it fails to account for the reason the person is asking the question. Broadly speaking, there are two kinds of questioners. There are questioners looking for answers, *and there are questioners looking for* exits; *that is, they're looking for reasons to abandon historic Christianity.*

The Deconstruction of Christianity, page 218

Read John 3:1-21:

There was a man named Nicodemus, a Jewish religious leader who was a Pharisee. After dark one evening, he came to speak with Jesus. "Rabbi," he said, "we all know that God has sent you to teach us. Your miraculous signs are evidence that God is with you."

Jesus replied, "I tell you the truth, unless you are born again, you cannot see the Kingdom of God."

"What do you mean?" exclaimed Nicodemus. "How can an old man go back into his mother's womb and be born again?"

Jesus replied, "I assure you, no one can enter the Kingdom of God without being born of water and the Spirit. Humans can reproduce only human life, but the Holy Spirit gives birth to spiritual life. So don't be surprised when I say, 'You must be born again.' The wind blows wherever it wants. Just as you can hear the wind but can't tell where it comes from or where it is going, so you can't explain how people are born of the Spirit."

"How are these things possible?" Nicodemus asked.

Jesus replied, "You are a respected Jewish teacher, and yet you don't understand these things? I assure you, we tell you what we know and have seen, and yet you won't believe our testimony. But if you don't believe me when I tell you about earthly things, how can you possibly believe if I tell you about heavenly things? No one has ever gone to heaven and returned. But the Son of Man has come down from heaven. And as Moses lifted up the bronze snake on a pole in the wilderness, so the Son of Man must be lifted up, so that everyone who believes in him will have eternal life.

"For this is how God loved the world: He gave his one and only Son, so that everyone who believes in him will not perish but have eternal life. God sent his Son into the world not to judge the world, but to save the world through him.

"There is no judgment against anyone who believes in him. But anyone who does not believe in him has already been judged for not believing in God's one and only Son. And the judgment is based on this fact: God's light came into the world, but people loved the darkness more than the light, for their actions were evil. All who do evil hate the light and refuse to go near it for fear their sins will be exposed. But those who do what is right come to the light so others can see that they are doing what God wants."

JOHN 3:1-21

13. Based on these verses, what principles can we glean from Jesus' interaction with Nicodemus that can help us in our interactions with people who are seeking truth and asking questions?

14. What are some helpful tips you can share about how to identify the questions behind a deconstructor's question?

In today's skeptical culture, it's not a matter of if doubts come, but when they come. So we need to teach Christians to doubt well.

The Deconstruction of Christianity, page 222

15. How can we teach Christians to doubt well? (See Matthew 11:2-5 for an example.)

Not every question gets a neat-and-tidy answer. That's because Christianity isn't tidy. There are formidable objections, difficult concepts, and troubling texts. There will always be some unanswered questions. That's not unique to Christianity, by the way. Every worldview has unanswered questions. The real question is, which worldview best explains reality?

The Deconstruction of Christianity, page 225

16. How do you cope with your unanswered questions? How might you help someone who is in the process of deconstructing to deal with their unanswered questions in a healthy and helpful way?

John the Baptist's story lays out a helpful strategy for addressing big theological questions. Don't ask people to ignore or suppress their questions. Instead, be the kind of person to whom people can express their questions. Do your best to understand their doubts while encouraging these friends and family members to keep them in their proper perspective. Help them frame their doubts as questions, and then search for good answers.

The Deconstruction of Christianity, page 226

17. Do you have Christian friends or mentors with whom you feel comfortable asking questions and even expressing doubt? If not, how could you develop this type of circle?

18. How might you create space for others to ask questions about their faith? How can you be part of the solution to the problem of church not feeling like a safe place to doubt?

19. What is one change you want to make after being in this study? If you can't answer this yet, set a time for your group to regather and answer this question after giving it more thought.

PRAY

Close your time together with prayer. You might want to take a little longer with your prayer time this week since it's your last meeting together. Invite group members to share things they are concerned about or hope to change as they move forward. Pray for one another as you continue your relationships with people who are deconstructing their faith. End with a simple prayer such as the one below:

Dear heavenly Father,

Thank you for this study and all the insights we've gathered from it. Help us to ask good questions and seek you for answers, both when we have doubts of our own and when we're interacting with those who are questioning their faith. Help us to be discerning about what's behind the questions we hear and then to respond with wisdom, grace, and truth. Thank you for welcoming us with our questions and complications. You are the Way, the Truth, and the Life. We love you, and we long for others to know you and love you as well. May it be so in the lives of those we know who have questions and doubts. Help them to find answers, not exits. Amen.

REFLECT AND TAKE ACTION

Maybe at this point you're struggling with the fact that you've reached the end of this book and your small group study, but your friend or family member—the reason you started this study in the first place—is still rejecting Christ. They've deconstructed, and none of your well-intentioned efforts made any difference. You were hoping for a settled outcome that hasn't happened.

Friend, that is not on you. Another person's spiritual journey is not something you can control. God is not expecting you to say the perfect thing in every situation, and even if you do have just the right words, the result may not be what you hoped for. God will accomplish his purposes; he isn't expecting you to be God. In fact, that's the whole point—only he can do what only he can do. Your failures will not make or break someone else's faith; that's not how salvation works. God is the one who saves, not us. He is the one who has the power to open someone's eyes to spiritual truth, not us. And he is the only one with the power to heal broken hearts.

That doesn't mean that you shouldn't keep on trying. The glorious truth of the gospel is that the Holy Spirit empowers us to carry out God's purposes in the world. We each have a role to play, and it's an important one. We just need to keep in mind that the results are not up to us.

This is a good time to assess the role God has for us in the lives of our friends and loved ones, in our churches, and in our spheres of influence. Let's go back one more time to the action steps we've been working on and ask some diagnostic questions to assess where we are and where we'd like to grow.

Pray

- Are you praying regularly for your friends' spiritual journeys? How could you grow in this area?

- Are your prayers Scripture based and gospel focused? How could you grow in this area?

- Do you have faith that God can do anything—
  even save the most hardened skeptic? Remember,
  Jesus answered the prayer "Help us, if you can"
  with "Anything is possible if a person believes"
  (Mark 9:22-23).

Stay Calm and Stay in Their Life

- Have you been trying to interact regularly with the
  people in your life who are struggling in their faith?
  If not, how could you rearrange your schedule or
  reprioritize things to be more intentional in this area?

- Do your friends feel comfortable sharing their
  struggles with you? If not, why might that be?

- Do you share your struggles with your friends— modeling vulnerability? What is something you haven't revealed that you should be more open about?

- Are you being patient with the process, trusting God to work in your loved ones' hearts and minds?

- Do you have a safe place to process your grief over your friends' struggles? This needs to be done carefully, of course, so you don't end up gossiping. But since the faith deconstruction of others can often feel like a death or a divorce, you do need to have somewhere to go with your own pain. And of course, there may be instances where it will not be possible or not be healthy for you to "stay in their lives." We recommend consulting a biblically faithful Christian counselor for help in discerning the right course for your circumstances.

Triage

- What are some good questions you can ask people who say they are deconstructing? Look back over your answers to the questions in this study guide for some ideas and gather them here so you can refer back to them.

- What are the particular issues your friends are dealing with? Spend some time praying for specific friends or family members and ask God to show you what you need to see. Then jot down what you think might be going on beneath the surface or what might need special care as you interact with them.

- What are some resources you might need as you help your friends walk through questioning or doubt?

Set Boundaries (and Respect Theirs)

- Where might you be crossing over someone's boundaries? Where might you be pushing too hard?

- Are there areas where you have been too cautious? Things you have been too afraid to bring up?

- Are there boundaries you need to set for your own spiritual or emotional health? How can you do that in a gracious and loving—but firm—way?

- Are there areas in which you have begun to compromise your own convictions to keep the peace? How can you love your deconstructing friend or family member and live by your convictions?

A FINAL WORD

We're so glad you've done this study with us, and we hope you've found it helpful. The most important thing is that you walk away with hope. Have faith in the God who can do the impossible and who loves us more than we can imagine. Trust that he is at work in ways we can't see. And know that the story isn't over until it's over. If you're living in the Saturday between the Crucifixion and the Resurrection, take heart. Sunday is coming.

A Prayer for Those Going through Deconstruction

Father in heaven, you are all-powerful, all-good, and all-loving. You know the end from the beginning. You know what lies deep in the heart and mind of my loved one, _____, who is in deconstruction. You know the causes, the confusion, and the circumstances that have led them to doubt the reality of your Word, your plan, and your gospel. I ask you to lead them to truth and heal all wounds. I ask that you use me in this process and give me wisdom to know what to say and when to say it. Shine your light on me and convict me if I have sinned against my loved one that I might repent and model that repentance to them. I trust you with my loved one and ask that you save them. Help me to trust you with this relationship, knowing that you work all things together for good for those who love you and are called according to your purpose. May the beauty of the gospel be on display in my life.

In Jesus' name, amen.

Notes

1. Greg Koukl, "Spiritual Warfare: Truth Encounters," *Stand to Reason* (blog), June 7, 2013, https://www.str.org/w/spiritual-warfare-truth -encounters.
2. Eve (@eve_wasframed), TikTok video, 0:07, October 18, 2022, https:// www.tiktok.com/@eve_wasframed/video/7155825175823519018.
3. Abraham Piper (@moreabrahampiper), TikTok video, 1:14, October 14, 2022, https://www.tiktok.com/@moreabrahampiper/video /7154426767363853614.
4. Mamatried (@erynjohnston), Twitter, November 17, 2022, 2:05 p.m., https://twitter.com/erynjohnston/status/1593334614818422784.
5. Blake Chastain, "'Exvangelical'—A Working Definition," *Exvangelical* (blog), March 2, 2019, https://www.exvangelicalpodcast.com/blog /exvangelical-a-working-definition/.
6. Lewis wrote, "I am trying here to prevent anyone saying the really foolish thing that people often say about Him: 'I'm ready to accept Jesus as a great moral teacher, but I don't accept His claim to be God.' That is the one thing we must not say. A man who was merely a man and said the sort of things Jesus said would not be a great moral teacher. He would either be a lunatic—on a level with the man who says he is a poached egg—or else he would be the Devil of Hell. You must make your choice. Either this man was, and is, the Son of God: or else a madman or something worse. You can shut Him up for a fool, you can spit at Him and kill Him as a demon; or you can fall at His feet and call Him Lord and God. But let us not come with any patronising nonsense about His being a great human teacher. He has not left that open to

129

us. He did not intend to." C. S. Lewis, *Mere Christianity* in *C. S. Lewis Signature Classics* (New York: HarperCollins, 1952, 2002), 50–51.

7. Neil Shenvi, "Sociology as Theology: The Deconstruction of Power in (Post)Evangelical Scholarship," Council on Biblical Manhood and Womanhood, November 21, 2021, https://cbmw.org/2021/11/21/sociology-as-theology-the-deconstruction-of-power-in-postevangelical-scholarship/.

About the Authors

Alisa Childers is a wife, a mom, an author, and a speaker. She was a member of the award-winning CCM recording group ZOEgirl. She is a popular speaker at apologetics and Christian worldview conferences. She is the author of *Another Gospel?* and *Live Your Truth and Other Lies*. She has been published at The Gospel Coalition, Crosswalk, the Stream, For Every Mom, *Decision* magazine, and The Christian Post. You can connect with Alisa online at alisachilders.com.

Tim Barnett is a husband, a father, an author, and a social media content creator. He is a speaker and apologist for Stand to Reason (STR). In addition, his online presence on *Red Pen Logic with Mr. B* helps people assess bad thinking by using good thinking, reaching millions of people every month through multiple social media platforms. Tim resides in the greater Toronto area with his wife, Stacey. They have three daughters and a Morkipoo.

Nancy Taylor has written or contributed to more than a dozen books and Bible products, including *God's Call to a Deeper Life* and *Doodle Devotions for Kids*. Her mission is to create resources that help people know God better, love him more deeply, and serve him wholeheartedly. She and her husband, Jeremy, have five children and live in Wheaton, Illinois. When she's not writing, editing, or doing mom chores, Nancy enjoys traveling and creating jewelry.

RECLAIM THE TIMELESS TRUTHS
OF HISTORIC CHRISTIAN BELIEFS

Another Gospel?—In a culture of endless questions, you need solid answers. If you have encountered the ideas of progressive Christianity and aren't sure how to respond, Alisa's journey will show you how to determine—and rest in—what's unmistakably true.

Another Gospel? DVD Experience—In this six-session series, Alisa will teach you how to use discernment, think logically, and make biblically based observations. This DVD experience includes in-depth interviews with *Cold-Case Christianity* author J. Warner Wallace and popular *Waddo You Meme??* YouTube apologist Jon McCray. Also available via streaming.

Another Gospel? Participant's Guide—This six-session workbook is designed for use with the companion *Another Gospel? DVD Experience*. This is a great resource for anyone wanting to explore the nuanced topic of progressive Christianity in a group or individually.

Rediscover Your Faith in a World Tragically Fascinated by Deconstruction

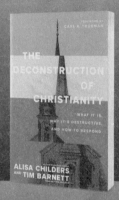

Understand the faith deconstruction movement and the best way to respond to it

A six-session series perfect for small group study

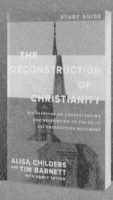

DVD to accompany the study guide with teaching from Alisa Childers and Tim Barnett

Also available via streaming